Greek Temples

Greek Temples

Don Nardo

Watts LIBRARY

Franklin Watts
A Division of Scholastic Inc.
New York • Toronto • London • Auckland • Sydney
Mexico City • New Delhi • Hong Kong
Danbury, Connecticut

Note to readers: Definitions for words in **bold** can be found in the Glossary at the back of this book.

Photographs ©: Bridgeman Art Library International Ltd., London/New York/British Museum, London: 38, 39; Corbis-Bettmann: 47 (Francis G. Mayer), 45 (Richard T. Nowitz), 16, 17 (Gian Berto Vanni), 5 left, 40 (Ruggero Vanni); H. Armstrong Roberts, Inc.: 27 (R. Kord), 22 (D. Lada), 49 (F. Sieb), 20 (A. Tovy), 34 (Key-Color/Zefa); Mary Evans Picture Library: 10, 29; North Wind Picture Archives: 13, 32, 42, 44; Photri/Bill Howe: 48; Robert Fried Photography: 5 right, 24; Stone/George Grigoriou: cover, 11; Superstock, Inc.: 14 (Pallas de Velletri), 8, 19, 37; The Art Archive: 28 (Dagli Orti/Fitzwilliam Museum, Cambridge), 31 (Eileen Tweedy/British Museum); The Image Works: 2 (Bill Bachmann), 6 (Sven Martson).

The photograph on the cover shows the Temple of Athena. The photograph opposite the title page shows the Temple of Apollo in Delphi.

Library of Congress Cataloging-in-Publication Data

Nardo, Don.
    Greek temple by Don Nardo.
       p. cm.—(Watts library)
    Includes bibliographical references and index.
    ISBN 0-531-12035-X (lib. bdg.)   0-531-16225-7 (pbk.)
    1. Temples—Greece—Juvenile literature. [1. Temples—Greece.] I. Title. II. Series.
NA275.N37 2002
726'.1208—dc21

2001022033

Contents

EQUAL JUSTICE UNDER LAW

The Supreme Court building in Washington, D.C., is a great example of the lasting influence of Greek architecture.

Chapter One

The Greek Temple Is Born

Today, nearly everyone is familiar with the **architecture** of large stone buildings whose entrances feature a row of **pillars** supporting a triangular **gable** beneath a slanted roof. This style of building design can be seen in banks, courthouses, and other important buildings all across the United States and Europe. One of the most famous examples is the U.S. Supreme Court in Washington, D.C. The structure's wide marble staircase leads up to eight soaring pillars, or

columns, which support its gable, called a **pediment**. The triangular space enclosed by the pediment is richly decorated with stone sculptures of larger-than-life human figures. So many modern structures use this architectural style that some people might easily make the mistake of thinking it was invented in modern times. In fact, though, the original versions of these buildings were the religious temples constructed by the ancient Greeks.

Today, Greece is home to more than 10 million people and covers an area of 50,949 square miles (131,957 square kilometers).

A Brilliant and Influential Civilization

Greece is a small, mountainous country that juts down from southeastern Europe into the warm and beautiful blue-green waters of the Mediterranean Sea. Today, Greece is a small country with a modest influence in world affairs. But, in

ancient times, Greece was the home of one of the most brilliant and influential civilizations in human history. That civilization, which created the splendid temples so admired and copied today, reached its peak in the fifth and fourth centuries B.C., about 2,500 years ago. Modern historians call that eventful and exciting period the **Classical Age**. In those days Greece was not a nation, as it is now, but was made up of a collection of city-states, each centered around a single city and a tiny nation in its own right in many ways.

Ancient Greece was the birthplace of many of the ideas and institutions that we take for granted today. Democracy and other important political systems, for instance, originated in ancient Athens, the wealthiest and most populous of the Greek city-states. The Athenians also invented the theater. And Greek thinkers, such as Socrates, Plato, and Aristotle, sought to understand the meaning of life and how the world worked. Their studies marked the beginnings of science and **philosophy**, the attempt to uncover the underlying meanings of life.

This illustration shows Plato teaching students at the Academy in Athens.

The Athenian Acropolis

The central towns of many Greek city-states were built around steep and often rocky hills that the inhabitants could retreat to—and easily defend—when danger threatened. The central hill was called an **acropolis**, meaning "the city's high place." The most famous example was the one in Athens, mainly because of the magnificent complex of temples and statues erected on its summit.

Among the other enduring contributions the ancient Greeks made to world culture was the design of the temples they built to their gods. The ruins of these once awesome structures are among the most popular tourist attractions for modern visitors to Greece. In particular, nearly every foreign traveler makes a point of going to Athens to see the remains of the Parthenon, which stands atop the city's central hill—the Acropolis.

Built in the late fifth century B.C., many experts now consider the Parthenon the most beautiful and perfect building ever erected. One early modern traveler was so moved by the sight of it that he remarked: "All the world's culture **culminated** in Greece, all Greece in Athens, all Athens in its Acropolis, and all the Acropolis in the Parthenon." Indeed, this majestic creation includes all the major features of classical Greek temple architecture. These features include four stone walls that form a rectangular inner shell and a row of stone columns, or **colonnade**, running along each side of the building as well as front and back porches composed of shorter colonnades and decorated pediments.

Worship in the Bronze Age

The huge stone temples displaying these features developed slowly over several centuries. In fact, the earliest Greek-speaking inhabitants of the region had no formal temples at all. Historians call these people the Mycenaeans, after Mycenae—one of their imposing stone palace-fortresses. Mycenaean ruins can still be seen on a rocky hill in southeastern Greece. The Mycenaeans lived in the Bronze Age, from about 3000 to 1100 B.C. The era is so named because the people used tools and weapons made of bronze—a mixture of copper and tin.

The Mycenaeans had several gods, including early versions of some of the gods worshiped later in classical times. These

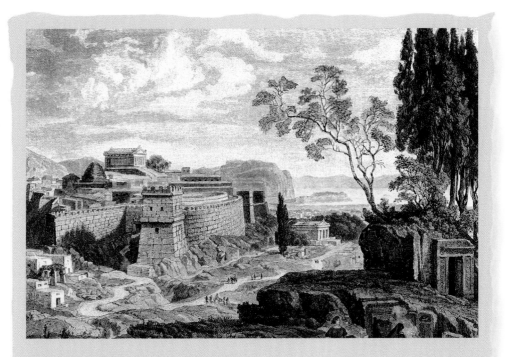

Mycenaean Palaces and Kingdoms

The Mycenaeans were great builders. To house their kings and royal courts, they erected many massive stone palaces that doubled as fortresses. Each was the center of a small kingdom. For reasons that are not well understood, these kingdoms declined and disappeared at the end of the Bronze Age, between 1200 and 1100 B.C.

included Zeus, leader of the gods, and Athena, his daughter, in whose honor the Athenians built the Parthenon. The residents of Athens, Mycenae, and other Greek towns in the Bronze Age did not make separate structures devoted to the gods. Instead, worshipers apparently gathered on certain mountaintops or in caves that they viewed as sacred spots. Or they set up shrines in tombs or in special rooms inside the royal palaces.

The Earliest Greek Temples

Following the collapse of the Mycenaean kingdoms, Greece entered a period that modern scholars call the Dark Age, which lasted for about three hundred years. It is called "dark" because civilization largely declined during that period. People stopped building palaces and other large stone structures. They were no longer able to read and write and most of the people were very poor.

One thing people did not lose in these bleak times, however, was religious belief. They continued to worship some of the old gods, along with some newer ones. At the same time, towns in isolated valleys and islands (which over time would develop into city-states) each adopted a particular god or goddess as its **patron**, or benefactor and protector. Athens chose Athena as its patron.

The residents of each town naturally wanted their divine patron to remain close to the community and watch over them. They reasoned that the best way to make sure this happened was to provide the god with a special house or shelter. In this way, the Greek temple was born. Because people thought that the gods sometimes actually lived inside their temples, these structures were viewed as sacred places. The surrounding grounds, where people set up altars

14

for worship, were also sacred. Together, a temple and its surrounding grounds made up the god's holy **sanctuary**.

These early temples were small, simple structures. They were essentially rectangular huts, each with a front porch having two thin columns and a pediment above them. They were also not very sturdy in comparison to later Greek temples. The walls were made mostly of sun-dried mud-bricks and the doorframes and columns were made of wood. The roofs were of **thatch**, or bundled plant stems and branches. These materials are highly **perishable**—they crack, crumble, or rot fairly rapidly. It is not surprising, therefore, that none of Greece's early temples has survived. Centuries would pass before the Greeks acquired the resources needed to erect stone temples, which proved to be far more permanent and impressive.

Local Patron Deities

Just as Athena was the patron goddess of Athens, the residents of Corinth (several miles west of Athens) chose Poseidon, god of the sea, as their patron. And Hera, protector of marriage, was the patron of Argos (a few miles south of Corinth).

This photograph shows the ruins of the Temple of Hera on the island of Samos in the Aegean Sea.

Chapter Two

Greek Temples Develop

Greece began to emerge from the Dark Age around 800 B.C., some three hundred years before the Classical Age began. In what historians call the Archaic Age (about 800–500 B.C.), local populations increased, people learned to read and write once more, **commerce** revived, and cities increasingly had the materials and ability to construct large buildings. The most dramatic example of such construction consisted of bigger, more elaborate, and more durable temples.

The first major change in temple architecture was to extend the two columns on the front porch into a full colonnade stretching all the way around the building. The first known temple to use this innovation was built on the Greek island of Samos in the early 700s B.C. and dedicated to the goddess Hera. The building was about 106 feet (32 meters) long and 21 feet (6.4 m) wide, and it had 43 columns in its colonnade. These columns were still made of wood because Greek builders had not yet made the transition to stone construction. But the temple was much larger and more complex than any that had come before, and it pointed the way to the future.

Turning to Stone

In the two centuries following the construction of the first large temple of Hera at Samos, Greek architects made many new advances. Perhaps the most dramatic and important one was the introduction of new roofing materials. Until that time, the roofs of temples were made of thatch or wood. These materials are relatively light so wooden columns and mudbrick walls were strong enough to support them.

However, in the 600s B.C., the builders started using roofing tiles made of **ceramics**, or baked clay. Ceramic tiles are extremely heavy. To keep the structures from collapsing under this added weight, the builders needed to build stone walls and columns. Stone is not only stronger, but also more durable. Using stone meant that the temples would last much longer.

By the mid-500s B.C., shortly before the Classical Age began, the transition from wooden to stone temples was complete.

The Doric Order

During the years of transition, Greek architects did more than develop stronger structural elements for their temples. They also experimented with ways to decorate these structures so that they would be more beautiful. Over time, various decorative elements came together into a standard style, or **order**. By the start of the Classical Age, the architectural style called the Doric Order came to be used for most temples built on the Greek mainland.

The columns of the Parthenon were done in the style of the Doric Order. Each column is topped with a capital and is marked with decorative lines, or flutes, along its shaft.

On this entablature, it is still possible to see traces of the reliefs carved onto the metopes. The triglyphs—sections with three lines or bars—are also clearly visible.

The aspect of the Doric Order that set it apart from other styles was the distinctive shape of its columns. First, the Doric columns had no decorative bases. Instead, they rested directly on the temple's stone floor, or **stylobate**. Even more important was the top, or **capital**, of the column, which consisted of two simple parts—a rounded stone cushion and a flat stone slab above it. The columns also featured **flutes**, narrow grooves carved **vertically** (up and down) into a column's stone shaft. Each Doric column had twenty flutes.

20

Another important feature of the Doric Order was the way the structural elements above the columns were decorated. The **horizontal** (side-to-side) section resting above the colonnade and holding up the roof is called the **entablature**. The entablature was usually about 3 to 5 feet (1 to 1.5 m) thick. On the entablature, directly above each column, was a block called a **triglyph**, which consisted of a cluster of three upright bars. The open spaces between the triglyphs were called the **metopes**. On these metopes, or flat panels, the builders placed either painted scenes or **reliefs**, sculptures partly raised from the flat surface. The paintings and reliefs typically depicted gods acting out scenes from well-known myths. Together, the entablature's triglyphs and metopes made up the temple's **frieze**, a colorful decorative band running around the whole building.

Achieving the Right Proportion

It became standard in the Doric Order for the height of a column to be from five to seven times its width. People thought this proportion was the most balanced and pleasing to the eye.

The Ionic Order and "Hundred-Footer"

While the Doric Order was developing on the Greek mainland, another architectural style—the Ionic Order—was also emerging. Ionic temples became popular on the islands lying east of the Greek mainland and on the western coast of what is now Turkey, which was then heavily populated by Greeks. Unlike Doric columns, Ionic columns have decorative bases. Also, the capitals of Ionic columns are more elaborate and elegant than Doric capitals. Each Ionic column is topped by two or more spiral-shaped scrolls called **volutes**. In addition, an

The volutes, or scrolls, are perhaps the most recognizable feature of the Ionic Order, as shown in this detailed photograph of the Erechtheum.

Ionic frieze has no triglyphs, so that it forms an unbroken decorative band running above the colonnade and below the roof.

The main goal behind the development of the Doric and Ionic orders was to make temples look as well proportioned and beautiful as possible. Architects came to believe that certain proportions did not look as pleasing to the eye as others. This was particularly true of the overall dimensions of the buildings. For example, the temple erected to Hera on Samos in the 700s B.C. was five times as long as it was wide. Such proportions eventually came to be viewed as awkward and unattractive.

By the dawn of the Classical Age, both Doric and Ionic temples had an overall proportion that seemed very balanced and attractive. Each temple was made to be exactly twice as long as it was wide. One of the first and finest examples was erected atop the Acropolis in Athens in the 500s B.C. People called it the "Hundred-Footer" because it was 100 feet (30.5 m) long. Like the Parthenon, which later replaced it, the building was dedicated to Athena, the city's patron.

Unfortunately, this imposing structure was destroyed by invaders shortly after it was built. At the time, no one knew that a new and far greater temple would rise in its place. Never in their wildest dreams could they imagine that the new temple would last for thousands of years and come to be viewed as a wonder of the world.

Mixing the Orders

Greek architects occasionally mixed the Doric and Ionic orders. They felt that adding a few Ionic features to a Doric building made it look more elegant.

Visitors appreciate the ruins of the Propylaea, an imposing gateway built around 430 B.C.

Chapter Three

Building Greek Temples

Almost everyone who travels to Greece today goes to Athens to see the Acropolis, the rocky hill that still dominates the city. Walking up the hill's western slope and onto the summit is an exciting and humbling experience. Near the top, visitors pass through the imposing ruins of a massive entrance gate—the Propylaea. Then the remains of the Parthenon come into view. Though now in ruins, this most famous of ancient temples is still a majestic sight. The

Parthenon's cracked, honey-colored stones form an impressive outline against Greece's deep-blue sky.

Walking closer to the temple, one is struck by two realities. First, it is a huge structure, towering some 65 feet (20 m) in the air. The temple is higher than three two-story modern houses stacked on top of one another. Second, its form and proportions are so flawless and beautiful that they approach perfection. These facts naturally raise the question of how the Greeks managed to erect such a magnificent structure. In particular, how did they build huge temples and other large stone structures without the aid of modern measuring instruments and machinery?

Cutting and Transporting the Stones

The first step in temple construction was to dig up the stones needed for the foundation, walls, and columns. For the Parthenon, an immense amount of stone—about 30,000 tons in all—was needed. The architects chose Pentelic marble. This fine white stone (now darker because of aging) was so named because it came from a quarry on Mount Pentelicon, about 10 miles (16 km) northeast of Athens.

In the quarry, the workers used chisels and **mallets** to cut grooves in the marble. Then they forced wooden wedges into the grooves. When they poured water on the wedges, the wood slowly absorbed the water and expanded, eventually causing the stone to crack. Finally, the workers slipped crowbars into the cracks to finish freeing the stones.

The Acropolis Complex

In ancient times, the Athenian Acropolis included three temples—the Parthenon, the Erechtheum, and the Temple of Athena Nike. In addition to these, it had a huge entrance gate, a storehouse for weapons, and numerous large statues and religious shrines and altars.

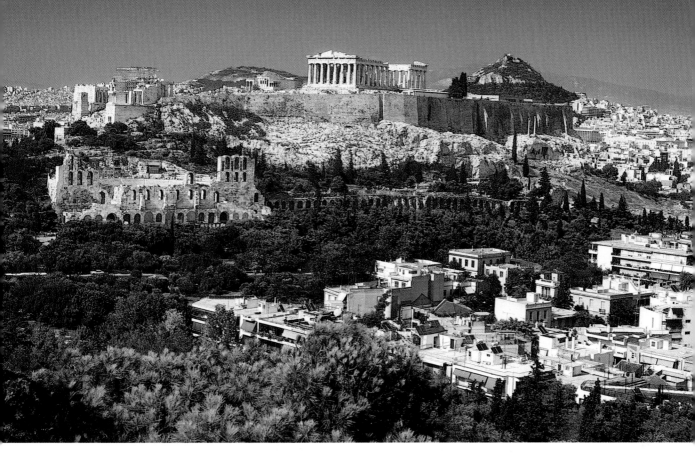

The next step was to transport the heavy stones down the mountainside and overland to the Acropolis. Gangs of workers used wooden **levers**, ropes, and brute force to get the stones onto wooden sleds and then dragged the sleds down the slope. On the level plain, the stones were transferred to wagons. The loads some of these wagons carried were so heavy that up to sixty oxen were required to pull them. Reaching the base of the Acropolis, the stones were transferred to sleds once more and this time dragged uphill to the work site on the hill's summit. These steps were very time-consuming. They were also expensive, because most of the hundreds of workers were not slaves, but free men who were paid each day.

To make the magnificent structures on the Acropolis, workers dragged all of the stones on sleds to the top.

27

Preparing and Placing the Stones

At the work site atop the Acropolis, teams of **masons**, expert stone carvers, prepared the unfinished marble blocks. To trim the stones, they used flat chisels, which they smacked with wooden mallets. Each stone had to be cut to fit exactly into a spot already measured by one of the architects' assistants. The stones had to be fitted very precisely because the workers used no mortar to join the stones. (The Greeks knew about mortar, a cement-like substance for filling cracks in stone structures, but rarely used it.) Instead, workers connected one block to another with iron clamps, which they inserted into the top of the stones. The next course, or layer, of stones covered the ones below, hiding the clamps.

Some of the masons cut rectangular pieces of stone for the building's foundation and walls. Others carved rounded

chunks of stone called **drums** to make the columns. Each of the Parthenon's columns consisted of about eleven drums stacked on top of one another, with a Doric capital at the top. A single drum weighed from five to ten tons. Lifting the upper drums into place was a daunting task.

Indeed, the higher the temple's stone courses rose, the more difficult it was to lift the stones. Today, builders use motor-powered cranes and other machines to raise such heavy loads. Lacking such advanced devices, the ancient Greeks relied on mechanical hoists, which utilized ropes and pulleys

This engraving shows ancient Greeks using ropes and pulleys to build the temples on the Acropolis.

attached to large wooden frameworks. They looped one end of a rope around the stone they wanted to move. Then they ran the rope through a pulley at the top of the framework and attached the other end to a team of oxen. When the oxen moved forward, they pulled the rope through the pulley and thus lifted the stone into the air. After the stone had been lowered into place, workers used crowbars to nudge it precisely into position.

The Frieze, Roof, and Cella

Once the colonnade and the walls of the inner enclosure had been erected, the next step was to construct the entablature—the horizontal section that holds up the roof—above them. First, the workers laid stone blocks horizontally on top of the columns to act as beams to hold up the rest of the entablature and the roof. Directly above these stones was the frieze, made of up alternating triglyphs and metopes. The Parthenon had fourteen metopes on each end and thirty-two on each side, for a total of ninety-two metopes.

Teams of sculptors carved scenes of mythical gods and heroes for the metopes. These artists followed sketches and

This relief was once a part of the west frieze on the Parthenon.

models prepared by an Athenian named Phidias, the greatest sculptor of ancient times. He also designed the larger stone figures that stood inside the pediments on the structure's front and back. These figures, as well as many other parts of such temples, were painted in bright colors, usually red, blue, and gold. Over the centuries, this paint faded and disappeared.

Above the entablature, the workers built the roof. First, they pieced together a sturdy framework of huge wooden

beams that rested on the tops of the walls and entablature. Smaller timbers overlaid the beams and the roofing tiles rested on top of the timbers. On the Parthenon, the roofing tiles were made of marble, so they were extremely heavy. Modern experts estimate that the building's roof weighed 3,000 tons!

One of the last steps in temple construction was to make a large statue of the god or goddess to whom the structure was dedicated. The statue stood inside the **cella**, a large room that occupied most of the temple's interior. For the Parthenon, Phidias designed a magnificent figure of Athena. The statue stood 38 feet (11.6 m) tall and was covered by sheets of gold weighing a total of 2,500 pounds (1,110 kilograms). Many years later, unfortunately, like all the other statues for Greek temples, this splendid creation was removed from the temple and dismantled.

The Metope Sculptures

The scenes in the Parthenon's metopes had various themes. Some showed gods fighting giants. Others depicted Greeks fighting Amazons—mythical women warriors—or **centaurs**—creatures that were half-man and half-horse.

Opposite: *The statue of Athena must have been an amazing sight to behold, as imagined in this engraving.*

Outside the temple, ancient Greeks would gather to honor their patron god through prayer and animal sacrifice.

Chapter Four

Temples and Religious Rituals

The people awake at dawn and dress in their finest clothes. Leaving their homes, they make their way through the streets, where they join hundreds of others. There is an air of festivity and excitement as they walk to the sanctuary of the city's patron god. Some of the people bring along animals that will be sacrificed in honor of that god. After gathering near one of several stone altars set up outside the temple, everyone prays and then watches a priest and his assistants sacrifice the animals. Then, in the shadow of the temple's towering colonnade, the people celebrate the god's special day by having a feast.

With a few local variations, this kind of scene was reenacted many times each year in every ancient Greek city-state. The Greeks were a very religious people who worshiped on a regular basis. Some kind of religious ritual accompanied birth, marriage, death, leaving on a journey, preparations for battle, athletic contests, and public meetings and ceremonies of all kinds. As the sacred houses of the gods, the temples were often the centers of such rituals.

The Great Procession

Modern scholars know more about the temples and religious festivals of Athens than those of any other ancient Greek state. This is because most of the surviving evidence happens to come from Athens. But it is probably safe to assume that similar festivals and rituals were held all across Greece.

Athens had many temples. But the two most important were the Parthenon and Erechtheum. Both stood on the Acropolis and both were dedicated to Athena, the city's patron. For these reasons, they were the focus of the city's greatest and most sacred religious festival. It was called the *Panathenaea*, which translates as either "All Athenians" or "Rituals of all Athenians." The festival was held every July, but the Athenians celebrated it on an extra-grand scale every fourth year. This occasion was so special, sacred, and colorful that it attracted visitors from many neighboring city-states. More than a hundred thousand people must have taken part.

The Panathenaea began with a large and stately procession, a march or parade, that began in the northern part of Athens. The marchers came from all social classes and groups. There were city leaders and elders, women, soldiers, children, slaves, and also **metics**—people born in other cities but who lived and worked in Athens.

Stepping to the music of flutes and drums, the marchers in the Panathenaic procession moved through the city's marketplace, the **Agora**. Then they climbed the stairs on the western side of the Acropolis. After passing through the enormous entrance gate, they proceeded to a huge altar that stood between the Parthenon and Erechtheum. The route that the great procession followed each year became known as the Panathenaic Way.

In Athens, people would fill the streets and walk to the temples on top the Acropolis as part of the Panathenaea celebration.

Presenting the Sacred Robe

Having reached the temples in Athena's sanctuary, the worshipers were ready to begin the sacred rituals. All such public worship took place outside the temples, rather than inside as happens in modern churches, synagogues, and mosques. At that time, people believed the gods resided in these structures from time to time. And worshiping inside their houses might violate the gods' privacy.

The first major ritual was the "presentation of the robe." The most important element in the entire Panathenaea was Athena's sacred robe, called the *peplos*. Each year a group of specially chosen young women wove a new robe for the goddess. This work was seen as a tremendous honor. Other chosen citizens carried the peplos in the great procession, and formally presented the sacred garment to a group of priestesses once they reached the temples. These women then carried the robe inside the Erechtheum. Later, in a different ceremony, they draped the peplos around the statue of the goddess that rested in that temple.

The statue of Athena inside the Erechtheum was made of wood from an olive tree. It was known as the *Athena Polias*, meaning "Athena of the City." According to legend, the goddess had once hurled the statue onto the Acropolis. And the people had erected the first version of the Erechtheum on the spot where the statue had landed to house the sacred image. That temple was eventually rebuilt several times. The ritual in which women gave the statue a new robe each year developed long before the advent of the Classical Age.

This relief shows the handing over of the peplos. On the left side, Athena is sitting with Hephaestos, the god of fire.

Sacred Sacrifices

After the peplos had been presented, the worshipers prayed and witnessed animal sacrifices to the goddess. In each Panathenaea, a hundred cows and many sheep and other animals were sacrificed. Such offerings followed strict rules and rituals. First, the worshipers draped garlands of flowers over the animals and led them, one at a time, to the altar. Then a priest or priestess poured water onto the altar to purify it.

The Temple of Hephaestos

Athens had many other temples besides the Parthenon and the Erechtheum. Among them was the Temple of Hephaestos, god of the forge, located on the western edge of the Agora. Today, with most of its colonnade and other structural elements still intact, it is the best preserved of all the ancient Greek temples.

Next, the person conducting the sacrifice stunned the animal by hitting it on the head with a club. Then he or she slit the animal's throat with a special knife, allowed the blood to drip into a bowl, and sprinkled some of the blood onto the altar. Finally, several priests cut up the animal. They burned the bones and fat, believing that the smoke rose up to the goddess and nourished her. Meanwhile, the meat from the animals was cooked and distributed among the worshipers, who held a ceremonial feast in Athena's honor.

Many other religious festivals in Athens had sacred processions and sacrifices similar to those of the Panathenaea. One of the most important was the Anthesteria. It took place in February in honor of Dionysus, the god who made the soil fertile so that plants would grow. Sacrifices were offered on the festival's first day. On the second day, a splendid procession marched through the town. A sculpted image of Dionysus—or an actor portraying him—rode in a wagon among the worshipers. On that day, it was customary for everyone, including children, to drink wine and for the children to receive gifts.

For centuries, the Greek city-states, which saw themselves as tiny independent nations, continued to fight among themselves, which eventually led to weakness and decline. Here, soldiers from the Greek states of Sparta and Syracuse slaughter a group of Athenians who have attacked Syracuse during the Peloponnesian War (431–404 B.C.).

Chapter Five

The Fate of Temples

The prosperous and powerful civilization that built the Parthenon and so many other imposing temples was not destined to endure. Beginning in the later years of the Classical Age, Greece entered a long period of decline. Because various Greek city-states and kingdoms repeatedly fought among themselves, they all became weaker and more open to attack from foreign powers. The biggest threat came from Rome, a strong nation based in Italy. In the second and first centuries

This engraving shows what the inside of the Temple of Olympian Zeus may have looked like at its peak.

B.C., a little over two thousand years ago, the Romans succeeded in overrunning the Greek lands.

During the centuries that Rome controlled Greece, the Greeks did their best to maintain the many temples that dotted their cities and countryside. Some fell into disrepair, though. And few new temples were built in Greece. The Greeks could no longer afford to erect such large and expensive structures. One notable exception was the Temple of Olympian Zeus, in Athens. This huge temple measured 354 feet by 135 feet (107 m by 41 m). It had double rows of columns on its sides and three rows of columns on its ends, each column towering to a height of 55 feet (17 m). A few of these columns still stand today, not far from the Acropolis.

The Temple of Olympian Zeus was financed by the Roman emperor Hadrian, who had a passion for Greek culture and ideas. In fact, even those Romans who did not like the Greeks were strongly influenced by them. The Romans adopted the style of Greek temples for their own temples and public buildings, for example. Eventually, Rome also went into decline. And after it fell about fifteen centuries ago, Greek and Roman temples all across the Mediterranean world began to fall apart.

Neglect, Earthquakes, and War Take Their Toll

When Greco-Roman civilization died out, no one cared anymore about keeping up the old temples. The people who now lived in Greece, Italy, and the rest of Europe were mostly Christians, and did not recognize the traditional Greek and Roman gods. As a result, some of the existing Greek temples came to be used for other purposes. The Parthenon, for instance, was used as a Christian church and remained so for some seven hundred years. Meanwhile, many other old temples were abandoned, and

The Greek-Loving Roman

Hadrian ruled the Roman Empire from A.D. 117 to 138, about six centuries after the Parthenon was erected. He studied Greek literature and philosophy and tried to restore some of the glory of ancient Greece. In addition to the Temple of Olympian Zeus, he built a new gymnasium and public library in Athens. He also restored many of the Greek temples that had been neglected.

they slowly cracked and crumbled or were destroyed by earthquakes or floods.

Partly because it was the most visible structure in Athens, the Parthenon managed to survive longer than most other Greek temples. In the 1400s, the Turks took control of Greece and turned the structure into a **mosque**, a temple where Muslims worship. In the west end of the cella, they erected a **minaret**, the slender tower common in Islamic buildings. For the most part, though, most of the building's original features remained intact, even after the passage of some two thousand years.

The Parthenon's days were numbered, however. In 1687, the Turks were at war with the Venetians (the inhabitants of the Italian city of Venice). The Venetians laid siege to Athens and bombarded the Acropolis with cannons and bombs. On September 26, a bomb hit the Parthenon and exploded some boxes of gunpowder the Turks had stored inside, turning the once-great monument into a ruin overnight.

The Parthenon Smashed

A Venetian who saw the destruction of the Parthenon left behind this eyewitness account: "One of [the Venetian bombs], hitting the side of the temple, ended by smashing it. The dreadful effect of this was a raging fury of fire and exploding powder and grenades, and the thunderous roar of the said ammunition discharging shook all the houses around. . . . And thus was left in ruins the famous Temple of Athena, which so many centuries and so many wars had not been able to destroy."

The Rediscovery of Ancient Greece

For a while, it seemed that the ruins of the Parthenon and other ancient Greek temples would continue crumbling and simply fade away. In the 1700s and 1800s, however, they began to enjoy an unexpected new lease on life. European and American scholars, poets, and artists became fascinated with ancient Greece, as the Roman emperor Hadrian had been. Many foreigners visited Greece and came back with excited accounts of the remnants of a once-great civilization.

This sculpture, along with several others, was removed from the Parthenon by Lord Elgin.

This longing for the past connected with ancient Greece had various outcomes. On the negative side, many foreigners removed some of the surviving sculptures from the ruined temples and took them back to their own countries. Perhaps the worst example was that of Lord Elgin, a British statesman. Between 1801 and 1812, he removed several of the remaining Parthenon sculptures and gave them to the British Museum. Many people later came to see his act as out-and-out theft.

A more positive result of the modern rediscovery of Greece's past was a deep admiration for Greek temple architecture. European and American architects began to copy this style in their own

The Parthenon in Philadelphia?

American architect William Strickland designed the Second Bank of the United States. The building's front and rear porches are exact replicas of those of the Parthenon, but on a smaller scale.

buildings. One of the most famous early examples was Philadelphia's Second Bank of the United States, completed in 1824. Hundreds of other banks and courthouses soon adopted the soaring colonnades and triangular pediments first introduced by Greek architects thousands of years earlier.

Another constructive outcome of modern interest in ancient Greece has been the attempt to preserve the crumbling temples and other relics of a glorious past. Restoration efforts occurred in the late 1800s and throughout the twentieth century. These increased in size and scope in 1975, when the Greek government created the Committee for the Preservation of the Acropolis Monuments. The ongoing goal of this group of architects, engineers, and scientists is to stop further decay of the Parthenon and Erechtheum. Similar groups across Greece are working to preserve other temples. The hope is that future generations will be able to admire and be inspired by these magnificent works of a vanished civilization.

Inside the Parthenon, cranes and scaffolding were used to help with some of the restoration.

Timeline

421–406	Near the Parthenon, the Athenians build the latest of several versions of the Erechtheum temple that houses Athena's sacred olive-wood image.
295	An Athenian tyrant named Lachares removes the gold from the statue of Athena inside the Parthenon and melts it down.
146	The conquest of mainland Greece by the Romans, conquerors of the Italian peninsula, is complete.
A.D.	
117–138	Reign of the Roman emperor Hadrian, who erects the Temple of Olympian Zeus in Athens.
ca. 400	The Romans remove the statue of Athena from the Parthenon and the figure subsequently disappears.
476	The last Roman emperor is forced from his throne. In the next century or so, Greco-Roman civilization in Europe declines and disappears.
ca. 1456	Athens falls to the Turks. Two years later they turn the Parthenon into a mosque.
1687	The Venetians, who are at war with the Turks, bombard the Acropolis and set off some gunpowder stored inside the Parthenon. The temple explodes, causing great damage.
1801–1812	England's Lord Elgin removes many of the Parthenon's remaining friezes and sculptures and ships them to London's British Museum.
1833	The Greeks drive the Turks out of Athens and establish the modern nation of Greece. Within months, archaeologists begin protecting and studying the country's ancient temples.
1970s–Today	Major restoration efforts increase and continue in an effort to keep the Parthenon and many other ancient Greek temples from further deterioration.

Glossary

acropolis—a central hill around which a Greek town was sometimes built. The word in ancient Greek means "the city's high place."

agora—a marketplace in an ancient Greek city

architecture—the art and science of designing buildings

capital—the top section of a column

cella—an ancient temple's main room, which usually held a larger-than-life-size statue of the god to whom the structure was dedicated

centaur—a mythical creature that was half-man and half-horse

ceramics—pottery, or baked clay

Classical Age—the term used by modern historians for the period in ancient Greece lasting from about 500 to 323 B.C.

colonnade—a row of columns

column—a pillar or a vertical shaft usually used to support parts of a building

commerce—trade and other economic activity

culminate—to reach the highest possible level

drachma—a coin that was the main unit of money in ancient Athens and many other Greek cities

drum—an individual section of a column in a Greek temple

entablature—the section of a Greek temple resting on top of the colonnade and beneath the roof

flutes (or **fluting**)—narrow grooves carved vertically into a column

frieze—a decorative band of paintings or sculptures running around a Greek temple on its entablature

gable—the triangular space located just beneath a building's slanted roof

horizontal—from side to side or from left to right

lever—a bar used to pry up a heavy object

mallet—a hammer with a wooden head

mason—an expert in carving and building with stone

metic—a person who had been born in another Greek state but who lived and worked in Athens

metope—a flat panel located between two triglyphs in the entablature

minaret—a slender tower common in Islamic buildings

mosque—a building used for Muslim worship

order—an architectural style or form in ancient Greece. The two main orders were the Doric and the Ionic.

patron—a benefactor, sponsor, or protector

pediment—a gable

peplos—the goddess Athena's sacred robe, which the citizens of Athens carried in the Panathenaic procession and draped around her statue in the Erechtheum temple

perishable—tending to crumble rapidly and therefore imper-manent

philosophy—the study of truth, wisdom, and the meaning of life

pillar—a free-standing vertical support to hold up a ceiling or roof

relief (or **bas-relief**)—a three-dimensional sculpture raised partly from a flat surface

sanctuary—a religious temple and the sacred grounds sur-rounding it in ancient Greece

stylobate—the stone floor of a Greek temple

thatch—bundled plant stems and branches, sometimes used to form the walls and roofs of primitive or simple structures

triglyph—a group of three upright bars placed directly above the top of a column in a Greek temple

vertical—up and down or from top to bottom

volute—a decorative spiral scroll on top of an Ionic column

To Find Out More

Books

Bowra, C. M. *Classical Greece*. New York: Time-Life Books, 1965.

Corbishley, Mike. *The World of Architectural Wonders*. New York: Peter Bedrick Books, 1996.

Jessup, Joanne. *The X-Ray Picture Book of Big Buildings of the Ancient World*. Danbury, CT: Franklin Watts, 1993.

Nardo, Don. *The Age of Pericles*. San Diego: Lucent Books, 1995.

———. *Life in Ancient Athens*. San Diego: Lucent Books, 2000.

———. *The Parthenon.* San Diego: Lucent Books, 1999.

Peach, Susan, and Anne Millard. *The Greeks.* London: Usborne, 1990.

Rutland, Jonathan. *See Inside an Ancient Greek Town.* New York: Barnes and Noble, 1995.

Organizations and Online Sites

Ancient Greece
http://www.mrdowling.com/701greece.html
This site has links to many sites with valuable information about the history and culture of ancient Greece.

The British Museum
http://www.thebritishmuseum.ac.uk/world/world.html
This site allows visitors to explore different world cultures, including Greece. Images of the museum's collection of ancient Greek artifacts can also be seen on this site.

Great Buildings
http://greatbuildings.com/gbc.html
This online site provides information and links to sites about many important ancient buildings, including several famous Greek temples, such as the Parthenon.

Greek Architecture

http://harpy.uccs.edu/greek/grkarch.html

This online site offers a general overview of ancient Greek architecture, with links to sites about various styles and periods.

The Greeks

http://www.pbs.org/empires/thegreeks

This site, built as a companion to the PBS television series, allows visitors to discover more about the people and history of ancient Greece.

The Metropolitan Museum of Art

100 Fifth Avenue at 82nd Street

New York, NY 10028-0198

http://www.metmuseum.org

The museum houses many artworks and artifacts from ancient Greece.

Odyssey Online

http://www.emory.edu/CARLOS/ODYSSEY/

This site contains a wealth of information on ancient Greece as well as other ancient cultures.

A Note on Sources

In writing this volume, I used two kinds of sources. I first consulted the primary, or original, sources, which is the standard procedure that historians follow. Primary sources are most often old letters, journals, poems, inventory lists, legal documents, and religious and other inscriptions carved into stone or some other durable material as well as chronicles written by ancient and other pre-modern historians. Such sources are not always as informative and reliable as we would like them to be. But they provide at least a partial picture of long-dead societies as drawn by the members of those societies.

In the case of the Parthenon and other ancient Greek temples, the primary sources are unfortunately fairly meager. Only a few descriptions of these structures by ancient writers have survived. The most important appear in a travel guide penned by a second-century A.D. Greek named Pausanias. Most of the information about ancient temples has come from the work of archaeologists, scholars who dig up and study ancient cities and artifacts.

Books and articles written by these and other modern scholars constitute the second kind of source I used. Known as secondary sources, they usually attempt to describe past events and people using information gathered from primary sources and physical examination of surviving sites and artifacts. This book about Greek temples is therefore a secondary source. Of the more advanced secondary sources I used in writing it, Peter Green's *The Parthenon* and A. M. Lawrence's *Greek Architecture* were particularly informative and helpful.

—*Don Nardo*

Index

Numbers in *italics* indicate illustrations.

About the Author

Don Nardo is a historian and award-winning writer who has published numerous books about the ancient world. Among these are *The Age of Pericles*, about the golden age of ancient Greece; *The Battle of Marathon*, which tells the exciting story of how the soldiers of ancient Athens defeated a much larger force of invading Persians; *Life of a Roman Soldier*, a fascinating study of the ancient Roman military; *Empires of Mesopotamia*, an overview of the ancient Sumerians, Babylonians, and Assyrians; and biographies of the great Roman general, Julius Caesar, and the wily Egyptian queen, Cleopatra. Mr. Nardo lives with his wife Christine in Massachusetts.